The Spirit of EARLY AMERICA

The Life and Words of Benjamin Franklin

The Old Academy buildings of the University of Pennsylvania.
(The Edgar Fahs Smith Memorial Collection, University of Pennsylvania)

Home Library Publishing Company
Fort Atkinson, Wisconsin

The famous sea battle between Commodore John Paul Jones's *Bonhomme Richard* and the English *Serapis* in 1779 was painted by Richard Elliot. (*U.S. Naval Academy Museum, Annapolis*)

The Franklin text for this book has been excerpted from *The Life and Writings of Benjamin Franklin*, edited by Albert Henry Smyth. Textual reproduction follows the Smyth edition, and spelling, capitalization and punctuation have been unaltered except where the original word might be misunderstood.

(Walters Art Gallery)

CONTENTS

B. FRANKLIN
PRINTER

Colonial Philadelphia, pictured by Norman Rockwell, was America's busiest and most exciting city during Benjamin Franklin's residence there. *(Collection of Mrs. Victor H. Neirinck)*

At an early age Franklin found that a quarrelsome attitude was worthless; only ignorant people resorted to it. He taught himself to write with strength and clarity and considered this ability as a principle means by which he advanced in life. At sixteen years he put his native wit to public use in letters to the editor of the *New England Courant*. His tongue-in-cheek letters from Silence Dogood, first of many pen names, gained him the respect of Boston's radicals who contributed to the *Courant*. When he was twenty-three, Franklin started his climb to popularity with his *Pennsylvania Gazette*. The paper achieved wide readership principally from the clever news stories, gentle satires and dialogues which filled its pages. His

INTRODUCTION

writing was always to a purpose — not the least of which was to entertain, but also to instruct and influence conduct. Franklin's unquenchable wit was two-fold good medicine: well-taken lessons for readers of his *Gazette* and *Poor Richard's Almanack* and much-appreciated income for his pocket.

His experiments in electricity and invention of the lightning rod (1752) were the accomplishments that first drew international attention to Franklin. European scientists considered Franklin the world's expert in this field. Franklin's contribution was scores of original experiments and observations, though he did not have the inclination to coordinate data into wider theory. The practical side of his genius was the first great manifestation of what was to become one of the continuing strengths of this nation. It lead to and was in many ways the model for America's impressive list of firsts — from the telegraph to the phonograph to the landing on the moon — in the fields of applied science and technology.

The wizard of electricity followed this fame with wider popularity for his *Way to Wealth* (1758), a compendium of sayings from *Poor Richard's Almanack* that are the most memorable expressions of the work-and-save ethic that helped build this nation and are now part of common speech: "Early to bed and early to rise, makes a man healthy, wealthy and wise," and if you would be wealthy, "Keep thy shop and thy shop will keep thee," and, "Wish not so much to live long, as to live well," to recall just a few.

During the long years as Pennsylvania assemblyman and years of negotiations in London (1757-75) and virtually running the U.S. embassy in Paris (1777-85), Franklin, the amiable country sage, was discovered to be a shrewd and bold diplomat. Franklin mixed politics with fearless humor by means of satire.

In London, before the American Revolution, he lobbied for American commercial and civil rights. The political essays written in defense of the colonies contain some of his sharpest wit and are quite bold in criticizing what he saw as injustice or pettiness of the King or Parliament. We are indebted to Franklin for his daring humor used in support of America. Though discontent and revolt in the 1770's seemed inevitable, Franklin

Of Franklin's many gifts, his genius as a calm, knowledgeable elder statesman greatly benefitted the young nation. In this Currier and Ives print, 1876, he stands with the drafters of the Declaration of Independence *(left to right):* Thomas Jefferson, Roger Sherman, Franklin, Robert R. Livingston and John Adams. *(Library of Congress)*

did much in writing and in person to maintain congenial ties with sympathetic Englishmen. Accumulation of untreated grievances radicalized him by 1775, and, back in America, he was a militant supporter of revolution. For his work in Paris which followed, he is given principal credit for securing money and supplies, without which the Revolution's success is doubtful.

A good example is the best sermon, as Poor Richard says. The best sermon on Franklin's genius is his own writing. This anthology of his writings is offered as an introduction to America's most agreeable genius. The biography of his life that emerges from the following excerpts of Franklin's writings may be astonishing when one considers the multitude of enterprises Franklin engaged in. The most amazing thing is that Franklin the man transcended them all. His genius lies in his happy balance of talents.

The childhood and early years of Benjamin Franklin are better known to readers around the world than the young life of any other of our Founding Fathers. Mark Twain complained that Franklin's example of early and sober industry has been a burden to altogether too many young boys in America. On the other hand, Franklin's early religious and sexual *errata* (as he called them) have been denounced as too tarnished a picture to pass for a good example. Whatever the judgments, everyone has heard that Franklin grew up as poor as a Boston church mouse, ran off to Philadelphia at seventeen with no more than a Dutch dollar in his pocket,

I EDUCATION OF A PRINTER

soon became one of that city's leading businessmen and scientists, and remained at the center of social and political affairs in America for three-quarters of a century.

We know so much about Franklin from his *Autobiography*, the most famous work of its kind in the English language. Franklin first set out to record his life in 1771, while resting at the English country estate in Hampshire of his friend, Jonathan Shipley, Bishop of Asaph. Here he wrote his history from 1706 to 1730 in the form of a letter to his son, William Franklin.

Franklin's style is easy and intimate, that of a poised old man, well-aware of and pleased with his world reputation, yet with a clear memory of his poor and obscure beginnings. His sprightly sense of humor is everywhere, beginning with his frank confession that he wrote his *Autobiography* in part to indulge his old man's vanity and talkativeness. We find his story much more than a mere how-to-succeed-in-business book. Franklin shows himself cheerful and eager, someone so approachable and whose successes seem they could be ours, if only we could learn his knack-genius.

Franklin's description of his parents indicates they were a good and stimulating influence. His formal schooling was brief — less than two years. The skills he became most talented in, masterful and persuasive writing and speech, were ones he taught himself.

At sixteen, after sensibly abandoning attempts at poetry, Franklin humorously began his literary career with his letters from Silence Dogood, fourteen in all, and published anonymously in his half-brother James's *New England Courant*. The brothers were not compatible, James being domineering and Benjamin defiant. Benjamin had received full discharge from his first indentures but still chaffed under his brother's rule. James, knowing he would leave if he could, insured that no other printer in Boston would give him work. Consequently, Benjamin decided to leave secretly so his family could not stop him. His trip to Philadelphia included a near-shipwreck off Long Island, a fifty-mile walk across New Jersey and about a ten-mile rowboat ride in October weather from Burlington, New Jersey, to Philadelphia.

An original printing press used by Franklin in Philadelphia, much like the one he learned on in his half-brother's shop in Boston, is on display at the Franklin Institute, Philadelphia.

Franklin in 1758 visited this small stone house in Ecton, England, which had been the ancestral home for centuries.
(American Philosophical Society)

Most people dislike vanity in others . . .

Autobiography, *1771*

. . . Having emerged from the poverty and obscurity in which I was born and bred, to a state of affluence and some degree of reputation in the world, and having gone so far through life with a considerable share of felicity, the conducing means I made use of, which with the blessing of God so well succeeded, my posterity may like to know, as they may find some of them suitable to their own situations, and therefore fit to be imitated.

Autobiography, *1771*

Hereby, too, I shall indulge the inclination so natural in old men, to be talking of themselves and their own past actions; and I shall indulge it without being tiresome to others, who, through respect to age, might conceive themselves obliged to give me a hearing, since this may be read or not as any one pleases. And, lastly (I may as well confess it, since my denial of it will be believed by nobody), perhaps I shall a good deal gratify my own *vanity*. Indeed, I scarce ever heard or saw the introductory words, *"Without vanity I may say,"* etc., but some vain thing immediately followed. Most people dislike vanity in others, whatever share they have of it themselves; but I give it fair quarter wherever I meet with it, being persuaded that it is often productive of good to the possessor, and to others that are within his sphere of action; and therefore, in many cases, it would not be altogether absurd if a man were to thank God for his vanity among the other comforts of life.

Franklin's birthplace on Milk Street in Boston is depicted in a nineteenth-century etching. *(The Bostonian Society, Old State House)*

Autobiography, *1771*

I think you may like to know something of his [Josiah Franklin's] person and character. He had an excellent constitution of body, was of middle stature, but well set, and very strong; he was ingenious, could draw prettily, was skilled a little in music, and had a clear pleasing voice, so that when he played psalm tunes on his violin and sung withal, as he sometimes did in an evening after the business of the day was over, it was extremely agreeable to hear. He had a mechanical genius too, and, on occasion, was very handy in the use of other tradesmen's tools; but his great excellence lay in a sound understanding and solid judgment in prudential matters, both in private and public affairs. . . . I remember well his being frequently visited by leading people,who consulted him for his opinion in affairs of the town or of the church he belonged to, and showed a good deal of respect for his judgment and advice; he was also much consulted by private persons about their affairs when any difficulty occurred, and frequently chosen an arbitrator between contending parties. At his table he liked to have, as often as he could, some sensible friend or neighbour to converse with, and always took care to start some ingenious or useful topic for discourse, which might tend to improve the minds of his children. By this means he turned our attention to what was good, just, and prudent in the conduct of life.

His great excellence lay in a sound understanding . . .

What is serving God? 'Tis doing good to man . . .

A View of Philadelphia, ca. 1718, by Peter Cooper, details the flurry of activity in the prospering port city that shortly would be Franklin's beloved home for the rest of his life. *(Collection of the Library Company of Philadelphia)*

Above: Penn's Treaty with the Indians, by Benjamin West, depicts the Great Treaty of peace in 1683 between the Quaker colonist William Penn and the Indians. Franklin found the same atmosphere of friendliness when he later entered Penn's colony. *(Pennsylvania Academy of the Fine Arts, Philadelphia, Joseph and Sarah Harrison Collection)*

Franklin borrowed books on writing and debate, read then overnight, if necessary, and returned them before his next day's work. *(American Philosophical Society)*

I had a strong inclination for the sea . . .

Autobiography, *1771*

. . . I was put to the grammar-school at eight years of age, my father intending to devote me, as the tithe of his sons, to the service of the Church. My early readiness in learning to read, which must have been very early, as I do not remember when I could not read, and the opinion of all his friends, that I should certainly make a good scholar, encouraged him in this purpose of his. . . . I continued, however, at the grammar-school not quite one year, though in that time I had risen gradually from the middle of the class of that year to be the head of it, and farther was removed into the next class above it, in order to go with that into the third at the end of the year. But my father, in the meantime, from a view of the expense of a college education . . . altered his first intention, took me from the grammar-school, and sent me to a school for writing and arithmetic, kept by a then famous man, Mr. George Brownell, very successful in his profession generally, and that by mild, encouraging methods. Under him I acquired fair writing pretty soon, but I failed in the arithmetic, and made no progress in it. At ten years old I was taken home to assist my father in his business, which was that of a tallow-chandler and sope-boiler. . . . Accordingly, I was employed in cutting wick for the candles, filling the dipping mold and the molds for cast candles, attending the shop, going of errands, etc.

Home for Christmas, by J.G.L. Ferris. This scene of colonial Philadelphia shows the wealth and charm the city emanated as the second largest in the British Empire in Franklin's time. *(Collection of William E. Ryder. Photo courtesy of Historical Times Incorporated, The Stackpole Company)*

I disliked the trade, and had a strong inclination for the sea, but my father declared against it; however, living near the water, I was much in and about it, learnt early to swim well, and to manage boats; and when in a boat or canoe with other boys, I was commonly allowed to govern, especially in any case of difficulty; and upon other occasions I was generally a leader among the boys, and sometimes led them into scrapes, of which I will mention one instance, as it shows an early projecting public spirit, tho' not then justly conducted.

Franklin's travel or lap desk, used on his widespread journeys. *(Franklin Institute, Philadelphia)*

There was a salt marsh that bounded part of a millpond, on the edge of which, at high water, we used to stand to fish for minnows. By much trampling, we had made it a mere quagmire. My proposal was to build a wharff there fit for us to stand upon, and I showed my comrades a large heap of stones, which were intended for a new house near the marsh, and which would very well suit our purpose. Accordingly, in the evening, when the workmen were gone, I assembled a number of my play-fellows, and working with them diligently like so many emmets [ants], sometimes two or three to a stone, we brought them all away and built our little wharff. The next morning the workmen were surprised at missing the stones, which were found in our wharff. Inquiry was made after the removers; we were discovered and complained of; several of us were corrected by our fathers; and, though I pleaded the usefulness of the work, mine convinced me that nothing was useful which was not honest.

Autobiography, *1771*

. . . I continued thus employed in my father's business for two years, that is, till I was twelve years old. . . . But my dislike to the trade continuing, my father was under apprehensions that if he did not find one for me more agreeable, I should break away and get to sea, as his son Josiah had done, to his great vexation. He therefore sometimes took me to walk with him, and see joiners, bricklayers, turners, braziers, etc., at their work, that he might observe my inclination, and endeavour to fix it on some trade or other on land. It has ever since been a pleasure to me to see good workmen handle their tools; and it has been useful to me, having learnt so much by it as to be able to do little jobs myself in my house when a workman could not readily be got, and to construct little machines for my experiments.

A printer's ink roller from Franklin's shop. *(The Franklin Institute)*

Autobiography, *1771*

. . . This bookish inclination at length determined my father to make me a printer, though he had already one son (James) of that profession. In 1717 my brother James returned from England with a press and letters to set up his business in Boston. I liked it much better than that of my father, but still had a hankering for the sea. To prevent the apprehended effect of such an inclination, my father was impatient to have me bound to my brother. I stood out some time, but at last was persuaded, and signed the indentures when I was yet but twelve years old. I was to serve as an apprentice till I was twenty-one years of age, only I was to be allowed journeyman's wages during the last year. In a little time I made great proficiency in the business, and became a useful hand to my brother.

Though pictured together in a late eighteenth-century print of France's favorite writers, Franklin was yet a boy in Boston while his fellow philosopher Voltaire *(left)* was already hailed a modern rival of Sophocles. Rousseau *(center)* was more nearly Franklin's contemporary. *(Metropolitan Museum of Art, gift of William H. Huntington)*

Above: Elfreth's Alley, Philadelphia, preserved much as it was in Franklin's time, was an area he probably saw when he entered the city as a very young man, though the cobblestones and street lamps were installed later as a result of his formative influence. *Right:* The Old Massachusetts Statehouse in Boston, now the oldest standing capitol building in America, was built during Franklin's childhood in that city.

America's first native sculptor, William Rush, also a Philadelphian, carved this wooden portrait bust of Franklin. *(Index of American Design and Decorative Arts)*

The exquisite pleasure of finding it met with their approbation . . .

Benjamin learned to compose type and print off sheets on the hand press in his brother's shop. *(Bettmann Archives)*

Autobiography, *1771*

My brother had, in 1720 or 1721, begun to print a newspaper. It was . . . called the *New England Courant*. . . .

He had some ingenious men among his friends, who amus'd themselves by writing little pieces for this paper, which gain'd it credit and made it more in demand, and these gentlemen often visited us. Hearing their conversations, and their accounts of the approbation their papers were received with, I was excited to try my hand among them; but, being still a boy, and suspecting that my brother would object to printing anything of mine in his paper if he knew it to be mine, I contrived to disguise my hand, and writing an anonymous paper, I put it in at night under the door of the printing-house. It was found in the morning, and communicated to his writing friends when they call'd in as usual. They read it, commented on it in my hearing, and I had the exquisite pleasure of finding it met with their approbation, and that, in their different guesses at the author, none were named but men of some character among us for learning and ingenuity. I suppose now that I was rather lucky in my judges, and that perhaps they were not really so very good ones as I then esteem'd them.

Encourag'd, however, by this, I wrote and convey'd in the same way to the press several more papers which were equally approv'd; and I kept my secret till my small fund of sense for such performances was pretty well exhausted. . . .

[*The papers Franklin refers to are the Dogood Papers. "Silence Dogood's" self-description follows. —Ed.*]

Opposite: Humorous letters from "Silence Dogood" to the *New England Courant*, penned anonymously by Franklin, arrived at the print shop while the young author overheard the approving comments. *(Historical Pictures Service, Chicago)*

A natural inclination to observe and reprove the faults of others . . .

From the Dogood Papers

To the Author of the New-England Courant, *1722:*

. . . *Know then,* That I am an Enemy to Vice, and a Friend to Vertue. I am one of extensive Charity, and a great Forgiver of *private* Injuries: A hearty Lover of the Clergy and all good Men, and a mortal Enemy to arbitrary Government & unlimited Power. I am naturally very jealous for the Rights & Liberties of my Country: & the least appearance of an Incroachment on those valuable Priviledges, is apt to make my Blood boil exceedingly. I have likewise a natural Inclination to observe and reprove the Faults of others, at which I have an excellent Faculty. I speak this by Way of Warning to all such whose offences shall come under my Cognizance, for I never intend to wrap my Talent in a Napkin. To be brief; I am courteous and affable, good humor'd (unless I am first provok'd,) and handsome, and sometimes witty, but always, Sir,

Your Friend, and
Humble Servant,

Silence Dogood.

[*When Benjamin Franklin was about 17, his brother James was censured by the Massachusetts Assembly, imprisoned for a month and ordered to no longer print the* New-England Courant, *in punishment for a political point made in the paper. It was decided in secret that Benjamin should be called the printer, that he should receive new and more liberal indentures from his brother, and the paper would go on. —Ed.*]

Autobiography, *1771*

At length, a fresh difference arising between my brother and me, I took upon me to assert my new freedom, presuming that he would not venture to produce the new indentures. It was not fair in me to take this advantage, and this I therefore reckon one of the first errata of my life; but the unfairness of it weighed little with me, when under the impressions of resentment for the blows his passion too often urged him to bestow upon me, though he was otherwise not an ill-natur'd man; perhaps I was too saucy and provoking.

When he found I would leave him, he took care to prevent my getting employment in any other printing-house of the town. . . . I was rather inclin'd to leave Boston when I reflected that I had already made myself a little obnoxious to the governing party, and, from the arbitrary proceedings of the Assembly in my brother's case, it was likely I might, if I stay'd, soon bring myself into scrapes; and farther, that my indiscrete disputations about religion began to make me pointed at with horror by good people as an infidel or atheist. I determin'd on the point, but my father now siding with my brother, I was sensible that, if I attempted to go openly, means would be used to prevent me. My friend Collins, therefore, undertook to manage a little for me.

The successes of his early writings multiplied when Franklin set up his own newspaper in Philadelphia. Artist Norman Rockwell painted him dashing off a piece for his *Gazette* or perhaps *Poor Richard's Almanack. (Collection of Mr. Joseph Hennage)*

Industry and frugality: perhaps Franklin overused these words — for he continued to remind people of them, even as a wealthy old man who no longer needed to practice them — and they tend to leave us with a distorted image of a penny-pinching workmonger. The fact was he retired handsomely after twenty-five years in printing and publishing, the last ten years of which he mostly managed and invested. Moreover he *lived* his *Poor Richard* maxim, "Wealth is not his that has it, but his that enjoys it." Franklin cared for wealth only as a means to secure leisure for scientific experiments and for public service, which he considered his duty.

When Franklin entered Philadelphia in 1723, however, industry and frugality, and a large measure of genius and common sense, were his only means to independence. He found a job with Samuel Keimer, printer, and began saving for his own shop. Governor Sir William Keith, a well-intentioned but inept ruler, patronized Franklin and assured him support

II PHILADELPHIA SUCCESS STORY

in his venture of becoming independent. Young Franklin believed his offers, and as his *Autobiography* accounts, set off for England with promises of letters of credit and reference from Keith to follow. Franklin found himself in London, deceived, without money or friends. He found a printing job, but spent his money on plays, amusements and "foolish intrigues with low women." He forgot his promises to Deborah Reed of Philadelphia, "attempted familiarities" with a Mrs. T—, "which she repulsed with a proper resentment," and lived from hand to mouth.

In a few months he returned to Philadelphia. Franklin started as a clerk, then signed again with Keimer until a co-worker's father agreed to set up his son and Franklin in printing. Franklin kept accounts meticulously, shrewdly cultivated acquaintances with those who might give them business and by 1729 began his *Pennsylvania Gazette.* At this time Franklin's partner sold out to become a farmer. Franklin prospered, gaining more subscribers to his witty *Gazette* with his satires printed under pseudonyms such as Anthony Afterwit, Celia Single and Alice Addertongue and his more serious essays on politics, morals and customs. He received government print orders, opened a stationers shop and began paying off debts.

In 1730 he married, without ceremony, Deborah Reed Rogers, who was technically married to but deserted by another man. She was thrifty and devoted, and together they thrived. Franklin's son, William (age six months to a year), became part of the household several months later. Franklin kept his own council, and no one has ever ascertained whether William's mother was Deborah or another. Deborah bore a son, Francis Folger, and a daughter, Sarah.

Nothing less than moral perfection became Franklin's next undertaking. With the modern tendency to disbelieve in absolutes, it is awesome to see the plan of someone who sincerely believed he could approach perfection. Franklin, relating this plan about forty years after in the *Autobiography,* gives the endeavor a perspective of humor and temperance, the first virtue for which Franklin aimed.

A happy result of Franklin's frugal, industrious years in Philadelphia was the success of his *The Way to Wealth*, or the preface to *Poor Richard's Almanack* of 1758, which was reprinted extensively. Many of his humorous hints for those who would be rich are contained in this 1859 engraving "Poor Richard Illustrated." *(Library of Congress)*

About this time, Franklin's wit found another outlet in the popular *Poor Richard's Almanack*, begun in 1732 and continued to 1757. Richard Saunders' almanac from the beginning outsold its competitors, and in fifteen years was a Pennsylvania institution, selling 10,000 copies a year and renamed *Poor Richard Improved*. To gain such popularity, Franklin had drawn on the wisdom and wit of the past sages and cultures. Under his scrutiny, the old lines were "pointed up," as he called it, sharpened and shortened.

ENGINE SIDE OF THE FRANKLIN ENGINE COMPANY
JANUARY 17, 1792
DAVID RENT ETTER ABOUT 1830)

Autobiography, *1771*

I have been the more particular in this description of my journey, and shall be so of my first entry into that city, that you may in your mind compare such unlikely beginnings with the figure I have since made there. I was in my working dress, my best clothes being to come round by sea. I was dirty from my journey; my pockets were stuff'd out with shirts and stockings, and I knew no soul nor where to look for lodging. I was fatigued with travelling, rowing, and want of rest, I was very hungry; and my whole stock of cash consisted of a Dutch dollar, and about a shilling in copper. . . .

Then I walked up the street, gazing about till near the market-house I met a boy with bread. I had made many a meal on bread, and, inquiring where he got it, I went immediately to the baker's he directed me to, in Second-street, and ask'd for bisket, intending such as we had in Boston; but they, it seems, were not made in Philadelphia. Then I asked for a three-penny loaf, and was told they had none such. So not considering or knowing the difference of money, and the greater cheapness nor the names of his bread, I bad him give me three-penny worth of any sort. He gave me, accordingly, three great puffy rolls. I was surpriz'd at the quantity, but took it, and having no room in my pockets, walk'd off with a roll under each arm, and eating the other. Thus I went up Market-street as far as Fourth-street, passing by the door of Mr. Read, my future wife's father; when she, standing at the door, saw me, and thought I made, as I certainly did, a most awkward, ridiculous appearance. Then I turned and went down Chestnut-street and part of Walnut-street, eating my roll all the way, and, coming round, found myself again at Market-street wharf, near the boat I came in, to which I went for a draught of the river water; and, being filled with one of my rolls, gave the other two to a woman and her child that came down the river in the boat with us, and were waiting to go farther. Thus refreshed, I walked again up the street, which by this time had many clean-dressed people in it, who were all walking the same way. I joined them, and thereby was led into the great meeting-house of the Quakers near the market. I sat down among them, and, after looking round awhile and hearing nothing said, being very drowsy thro' labour and want of rest the preceding night, I fell fast asleep, and continu'd so till the meeting broke up, when one was kind enough to rouse me. This was, therefore, the first house I was in, or slept in, in Philadelphia.

Observe all men, thyself the most . . .

Opposite: Franklin's amusing appearance as he entered Philadelphia was painted by David Rent Etter on the decorative side panel of a fire engine, as was the style for such machines. *(Insurance Company of North America)*

A montage of Franklin's printing tools from his shop includes typesetting *(center)* and type dressing *(right)* tables, printing press *(rear)* ink pads and roller, composing sticks, mallet and block. *(Franklin Institute, Philadelphia)*

I took care to appear industrious and frugal . . .

Autobiography, *1771*

. . . In order to secure my credit and character as a tradesman, I took care not only to be in *reality* industrious and frugal, but to avoid all appearances to the contrary. I drest plainly; I was seen at no places of idle diverson. I never went out a fishing or shooting; a book, indeed, sometimes debauch'd me from my work, but that was seldom, snug, and gave no scandal; and, to show that I was not above my business, I sometimes brought home the paper I purchas'd at the stores thro' the streets on a wheelbarrow. Thus being esteem'd an industrious, thriving young man, and paying duly for what I bought, the merchants who imported stationery solicited my custom; others proposed supplying me with books, and I went on swimmingly. In the mean time, Keimer's credit and business declining daily, he was at last forc'd to sell his printing-house to satisfy his creditors. He went to Barbadoes, and there lived some years in very poor circumstances. . . .

There remained now no competitor with me at Philadelphia but the old one, Bradford; who was rich and easy, did a little print-

Franklin made a point of looking the industrious tradesman
when he opened his own printing shop in 1728 in Philadelphia at the young age of 22.
(Historical Pictures Service, Chicago)

A good wife and health, is a man's best wealth . . .

Deborah Reed became Franklin's wife in September 1730, a marriage that lasted 44 companionable years. Because of his absences in London over the course of 15 years, Franklin commissioned Benjamin Wilson to paint this portrait of Deborah and one of himself to be hung together in their Philadelphia home. *(American Philosophical Society)*

ing now and then by straggling hands, but was not very anxious about the business. However, as he kept the post-office, it was imagined he had better opportunities of obtaining news; his paper was thought a better distributor of advertisements than mine, and therefore had many more, which was a profitable thing to him, and a disadvantage to me; for, tho' I did indeed receive and send papers by the post, yet the publick opinion was otherwise, for what I did send was by bribing the riders, who took them privately, Bradford being unkind enough to forbid it, which occasion'd some resentment on my part; and I thought so meanly of him for it, that, when I afterward came into his situation, I took care never to imitate it.

Autobiography, *1771*

. . . Having turned my thoughts to marriage, I look'd round me and made overtures of acquaintance in other places; but soon found that, the business of a printer being generally thought a poor one, I was not to expect money with a wife, unless with such a one as I should not otherwise think agreeable. In the mean time, that hard-to-be-governed passion of youth hurried me frequently into intrigues with low women that fell in my way, which were attended with some expense and great inconvenience, besides a continual risque to my health by a distemper which of all things I dreaded, though by great good luck I escaped it. A friendly correspondence as neighbours and old acquaintances had continued between me and Mrs. Read's family, who all had a regard for me from the time of my first lodging in their house. I was often invited there and consulted in their affairs, wherein I sometimes was of service. I piti'd poor Miss Read's unfortunate situation, who was generally dejected, seldom chearful, and avoided company. I considered my giddiness and inconstancy when in London as in a great degree the cause of her unhappiness, tho' the mother was good enough to think the fault more her own than mine, as she had prevented our marrying before I went thither, and persuaded the other match in my absence. Our mutual affection was revived, but there were now great objections to our union. The match was indeed looked upon as invalid, a preceding wife [of Deborah Read's first husband, who deserted her in 1727 or 1728] being said to be living in England; but this could not easily be prov'd, because of the distance; and, tho' there was a report of his death, it was not certain. Then, tho' it should be true, he had left many debts, which his successor might be call'd upon to pay. We ventured, however, over all these difficulties, and I took her to wife, September 1st, 1730. None of the inconveniences happened that we had apprehended; she proved a good and faithful helpmate, assisted me much by attending the shop; we throve together, and have ever mutually endeavor'd to make each other happy. Thus I corrected that great *erratum* as well as I could.

Autobiography, *France, 1784*

It was about this time I conceiv'd the bold and arduous project of arriving at moral perfection. I wish'd to live without committing any fault at any time; I would conquer all that either natural inclination, custom, or company might lead me into. As I knew, or thought

The bold and arduous project of arriving at moral perfection . . .

The Philadelphia artist Charles Willson Peale painted Franklin's portrait about 1758, capturing the aura of benevolence and tranquility for which Franklin aimed in his plan for moral perfection. *(Pennsylvania Academy of the Fine Arts, Joseph and Sarah Harrison Collection)*

Speak not but what may benefit others or yourself . . .

I knew, what was right and wrong, I did not see why I might not always do the one and avoid the other. But I soon found I had undertaken a task of more difficulty than I had imagined. While my care was employ'd in guarding against one fault, I was often surprised by another; habit took the advantage of inattention; inclination was sometimes too strong for reason. I concluded, at length, that the mere speculative conviction that it was our interest to be completely virtuous, was not sufficient to prevent our slipping; and that the contrary habits must be broken, and good ones acquired and established, before we can have any dependence on a steady, uniform rectitude of conduct. For this purpose I therefore contrived the following method.

In the various enumerations of the moral virtues I had met with in my reading, I found the catalogue more or less numerous. . . . I propos'd to myself, for the sake of clearness, to use rather more names, with fewer ideas annex'd to each, than a few names with more ideas; and I included under thirteen names of virtues all that at that time occurr'd to me as necessary or desirable, and annexed to each a short precept, which fully express'd the extent I gave to its meaning.

These names of virtues, with their precepts, were:

1. Temperance

Eat not to dullness; drink not to elevation.

2. Silence

Speak not but what may benefit others or yourself; avoid trifling conversation.

3. Order

Let all your things have their places; let each part of your business have its time.

4. Resolution

Resolve to perform what you ought; perform without fail what you resolve.

5. Frugality

Make no expense but to do good to others or yourself; *i.e.*, waste nothing.

6. Industry

Lose no time; be always employ'd in something useful; cut off all unnecessary actions.

7. Sincerity

Use no hurtful deceit; think innocently and justly, and, if you speak, speak accordingly.

8. Justice

Wrong none by doing injuries, or omitting the benefits that are your duty.

9. Moderation

Avoid extreams; forbear resenting injuries so much as you think they deserve.

10. Cleanliness

Tolerate no uncleanliness in body, clothes, or habitation.

11. Tranquility

Be not disturbed at trifles, or at accidents common or unavoidable.

Above: High Street, Philadelphia, was the area in which Franklin settled, upon his return to the city in 1762. His business and home were built along this street. *(Historical Society of Pennsylvania)*

Right: A maxim from "Poor Richard Illustrated": Creditors have better memories than debtors. *(Library of Congress)*

"Sunny, good for haying."
Almanack
There's more
old Drunkard
than old Do
One good Husband is worth two good Wives; for the scarcer things are, the more they'r valued.
Love your Neighbour; yet don't pull down your Hedge.
The Golden Age was never the present Age.

The year 1733 saw the first of the incomparable *Poor Richard's Almanacks,* which, over the 25 years of their publication, became a Pennsylvania institution that farmers, businessmen, matrons, lovers and politicians alike looked forward to.
(Norman Rockwell painting from the collection of Mr. Joseph Hennage)

It is hard for an empty sack to stand upright . . .

12. Chastity

Rarely use venery but for health or offspring, never to dullness, weakness, or the injury of your own or another's peace or reputation.

13. Humility

Imitate Jesus and Socrates.

My intention being to acquire the *habitude* of all these virtues, I judg'd it would be well not to distract my attention by attempting the whole at once, but to fix it on one of them at a time; and, when I should be master of that, then to proceed to another, and so on, till I should have gone thro' the thirteen; and, as the previous acquisition of some might facilitate the acquisition of certain others, I arrang'd them with that view, as they stand above. . . .

Franklin at a desk, by David Rent Etter, from the side panel of a hand pump engine. *(Insurance Company of North America)*

Autobiography, *1788*

In 1732 I first publish'd my Almanack, under the name of *Richard Saunders*; it was continu'd by me about twenty-five years, commonly call'd *Poor Richard's Almanack.* I endeavour'd to make it both entertaining and useful, and it accordingly came to be in such demand, that I reap'd considerable profit from it, vending annually near ten thousand. And observing that it was generally read, scarce any neighborhood in the province being without it, I consider'd it as a proper vehicle for conveying instruction among the common people, who bought scarcely any other books; I therefore filled all the little spaces that occurr'd between the remarkable days in the calendar with proverbial sentences, chiefly such as inculcated industry and frugality, as the means of procuring wealth, and thereby securing virtue; it being more difficult for a man in want, to act always honestly, as, to use here one of those proverbs, *it is hard for an empty sack to stand upright.*

These proverbs, which contained the wisdom of many ages and nations, I assembled and form'd into a connected discourse prefix'd to the Almanack of 1757, as the harangue of a wise old man to the people attending an auction. The bringing all these scatter'd counsels thus into a focus enabled them to make a greater impression.

From the preface to Poor Richard's Almanack, *1733*

Courteous Reader,

I might in this place attempt to gain thy Favour, by declaring that I write Almanacks with no other View than that of the publick Good; but in this I should not be sincere; and Men are now adays too wise to be deceiv'd by Pretences how specious soever. The Plain Truth of the Matter is, I am excessive poor, and my Wife, good Woman, is, I tell her, excessive proud; she cannot bear, she says, to sit spinning in her Shift of Tow, while I do nothing but gaze at the Stars; and has threatned more than once to burn all my Books and Rattling-Traps (as she calls my Instruments) if I do not make some profitable Use of them for the Good of my Family. The Printer has offer'd me some considerable share of the Profits, and I have thus begun to comply with my Dame's Desire.

Likenesses of Franklin were widely reproduced during his life and posthumously on snuffboxes, bottles, mugs, miniature busts and even wooden hats. *(Index of American Design and Decorative Arts)*

N°. 32

Mural by Thornton Oakley, in the Lecture Hall of the Franklin Institute, Philadelphia.

Opposite: The Green Tree fire mark, 1784, identified homes insured against fire by the Mutual Assurance Company. In the early days of fire fighting, if the company that first arrived on the scene of a fire was not the one with which the house was insured, the firemen let it burn. By the 1760's in Philadelphia, however, companies cooperated. *(Index of American Design and Decorative Arts)*

Sloth makes all things difficult, but industry all easy . . .

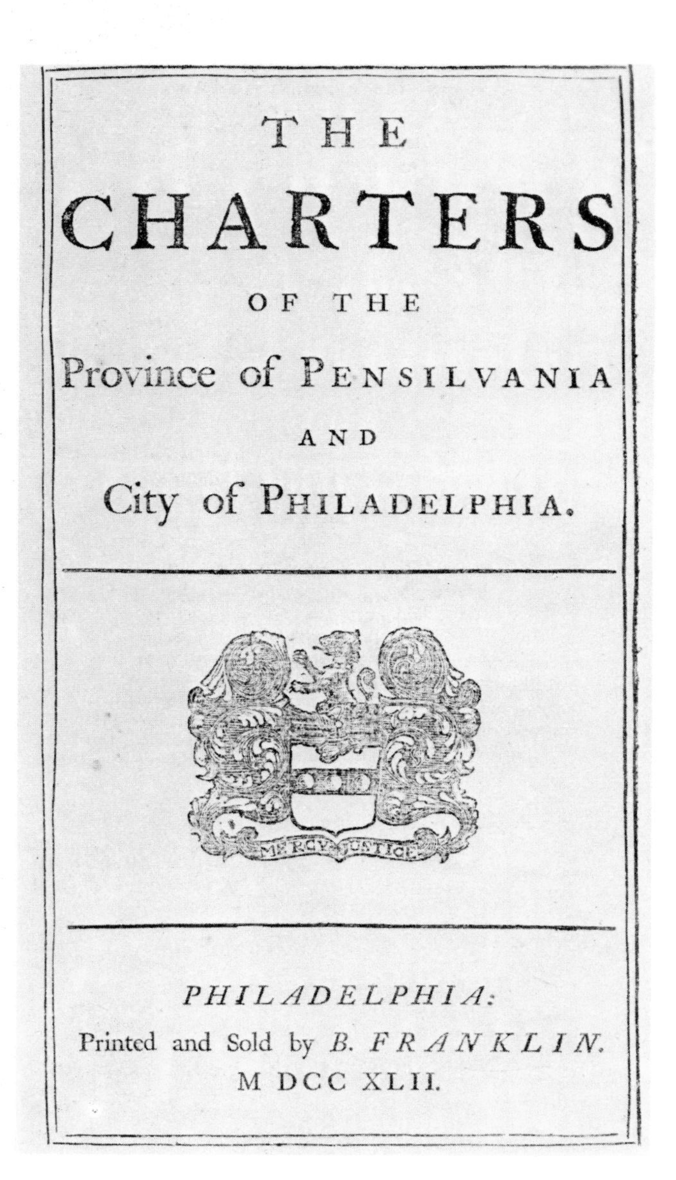
THE

CHARTERS

OF THE

Province of PENSILVANIA

AND

City of PHILADELPHIA.

PHILADELPHIA:

Printed and Sold by *B. FRANKLIN.*

M DCC XLII.

One of the profitable jobs that Franklin secured from his contacts in the Assembly was printing the colonial charters.
(Insurance Company of North America)

Autobiography, *1788*

My first promotion was my being chosen, in 1736, clerk of the General Assembly. The choice was made that year without opposition; but the year following, when I was again propos'd (the choice, like that of the members, being annual), a new member made a long speech against me, in order to favour some other candidate. I was, however, chosen, which was the more agreeable to me, as, besides the pay for the immediate service as clerk, the place gave me a better opportunity of keeping up an interest among the members, which secur'd to me the business of printing the votes, laws, paper money, and other occasional jobbs for the public, that, on the whole, were very profitable.

[French and Indian attacks had continued on the western frontier of Pennsylvania, and a well publicized attack was the burning and massacre of the Moravian village of Gnadenhut. In 1756, when Franklin was fifty years old, the governor asked him to lead a troop of men there to build a line of forts. He soon raised 560 volunteers and set out with his son William, an officer. —Ed.]

The officers of Franklin's regiment surprised and embarrassed him once by escorting him for a short distance, while mounted, in uniform and with swords drawn. Print from Holley's *The Life of Benjamin Franklin, 1848. (Benjamin Franklin Collection, Yale University Library)*

A life of leisure and a life of laziness are two things . . .

Autobiography, *1788*

It was the beginning of January when we set out upon this business of building forts. . . . We continu'd our march, and arriv'd at the desolated Gnadenhut. There was a sawmill near, round which were left several piles of boards, with which we soon hutted ourselves; an operation the more necessary at that inclement season, as we had no tents. Our first work was to bury more effectually the dead we found there, who had been half interr'd by the country people.

A little neglect may breed great mischief . . .

The next morning our fort was plann'd and mark'd out, the circumference measuring four hundred and fifty-five feet, which would require as many palisades to be made of trees, one with another, of a foot diameter each. Our axes, of which we had seventy, were immediately set to work to cut down trees, and, our men being dextrous in the use of them, great despatch was made. . . . While these were preparing, our other men dug a trench all round, of three feet deep, in which the palisades were to be planted; and, our waggons, the bodys being taken off, and the fore and hind wheels separated by taking out the pin which united the two parts of the perch, we had ten carriages, with two horses each, to bring the palisades from the woods to the spot. When they were set up, our carpenters built a stage of boards all round within, about six feet high, for the men to stand on when to fire thro' the loopholes. We had one swivel gun, which we mounted on one of the angles, and fir'd it as soon as fix'd, to let the Indians know, if any were within hearing, that we had such pieces; and thus our fort, if such a magnificent name may be given to so miserable a stockade, was finish'd in a week, though it rain'd so hard every other day that the men could not work. . . .

This kind of fort, however contemptible, is a sufficient defense against Indians, who have no cannon.

Finding ourselves now posted securely, and having a place to retreat to on occasion, we ventur'd out in parties to scour the adjacent country. We met with no Indians, but we found the places on the neighbouring hills where they had lain to watch our proceedings. There was an art in their contrivance of those places that seems worth mention. It being winter, a fire was necessary for them; but a common fire on the surface of the ground would by its light have discover'd their position at a distance. They had therefore dug holes in the ground about three feet diameter, and somewhat deeper; we saw where they had with their hatchets cut off the charcoal from the sides of burnt logs lying in the woods. With these coals they had made small fires in the bottom of the holes, and we observ'd among the weeds and grass the prints of their bodies, made by their laying all round, with their legs hanging down in the holes to keep their feet warm, which, with them, is an essential point. This kind of fire, so manag'd, could not discover them, either by its light, flame, sparks, or even smoke.

One of the earliest portraits of Franklin,
painted between 1738-46 and attributed to Robert Feke,
shows him about the time he invented his famous stove
and began experimenting with electricity.
(Fogg Art Museum, Harvard University)

"For my own Part, when I am employed in serving others, I do not look upon myself as conferring Favours, but as paying Debts. In my Travels, and since my Settlement, I have received much Kindness from Men, to whom I shall never have any Opportunity of making the least direct Return . . . I can therefore only Return on their Fellow Men; and I can only show my Gratitude for these mercies from God, by a readiness to help his other Children and my Brethren."

Franklin's words to a friend in Pennsylvania, Joseph Huey, best explain his attitude not only toward what he considered his civic duties, but also his investigations as scientist, or philosopher, as the term was used in the eighteenth century. During the time he reserved for study, he made some of the most famous and most practical discoveries of his time.

Nearly every American gradeschooler learns of his famous experiments with the kite and electricity. Even in his time he was famous among scientists as the world's foremost expert on electricity. To sum-

III AMERICA'S FOREMOST INVENTOR

marize briefly his discoveries in this field: The most important concepts were the existence of *positive* and *negative* electricity, the fluidity of electricized particles and the identity of lightning and electricity — the last proved by the kite experiment related in this chapter. Franklin also invented and named the battery from his experiments with the Leyden jar, and his electrical experiments were performed and confirmed all over the world scientific community. His suggestion and practical device for protecting houses from lightning was another first. For his work, he was elected to the English Royal Academy of Sciences in 1756.

Other practical inventions were the lightning rod, bifocals, a flexible catheter, an armchair that converted to library stepladder and a device for removing books from high shelves, all of which came about as solutions to ordinary needs. His insatiable curiosity about everyday phenomena went in wider directions. Letters to fellow scientists include observations on the effect of oil on water, the cause of the aurora borealis (northern lights), causes and cures of smoky chimneys, the relationship of tobacco to hand tremors, effects of diet and activity on general health, depth of water and speed of boats, the course of the Gulf Stream and its effects on shipping, the southwest origin of our northeast storms and more! In sum, his curiosity touched on nearly every eighteenth-century intellectual pursuit.

Among personal accomplishments, he designed (based on previous plans), built and played the harmonica and also played the harp, guitar and violin. He taught himself a reading knowledge of French, Italian, Spanish, German and Latin. His lifelong interest in medicine and health was acknowledged in his election to the Royal Medical Society of Paris and honorary membership in the Medical Society of London. In his business of printing, of course, he was expert in knowledge of ink, typefaces and paper and kept close business and personal relations with the King's printer, William Strahan. In his own words, Benjamin Franklin was "quite a factotum" — with a charge of genius.

Benjamin Franklin of Philadelphia, 1761, mezzotint by James McArdell.
Franklin the scientist stands surrounded by symbols of his work: a book marked *Electric Exp.*, a static electricity machine with glass globe *(right)* and lightning in the background.
(New York Public Library)

A South-East Prospect of the Pensylvania
This Building, by the Bounty of the Government, And of many private

A South-East Prospect of the Pennsylvania Hospital with the Elevation of the Intended Plan, engraved by H. Dawkins. Dr. Thomas Bond with Franklin's help began the Pennsylvania Hospital in 1751. *(Courtesy, Henry Francis du Pont Winterthur Museum, Joseph Downs Manuscript Collection.)*

Above: Franklin, with his son William, carried on the famous kite experiment in 1752 which equated lightning with electricity. (Engine side, *Insurance Company of North America*) *Opposite:* A highly imaginative painting, *Benjamin Franklin Drawing Electricity from the Sky,* ca. 1805, by Benjamin West, shows him an old sage seated on clouds, his electrical apparatus to the left and several cherubs to the right aiding him by flying the kite while he touches his knuckle to the electricized key. *(Philadelphia Museum of Art, Mr. and Mrs. Wharton Sinkler Collection)*

What signifies Philosophy [science] that does not apply to some use? . . .

From Experiments and Observation on Electricity *(Electrical Kite)*
To Peter Collinson, 1752

Sir: As frequent mention is made in public papers from *Europe* of the success of the *Philadelphia* experiment for drawing the electric fire from clouds by means of pointed rods of iron erected on high buildings, &c., it may be agreeable to the curious to be informed, that the same experiment has succeeded in *Philadelpha*, though made in a different and more easy manner, which is as follows:

Make a small cross of two light strips of cedar, the arms so long as to reach to the four corners of a large thin silk handkerchief when extended; tie the corners of the handkerchief to the extremities of the cross, so you have the body of a kite; which being properly accommodated with a tail, loop, and string, will rise in the air, like those made of paper; but this being of silk, is fitter to bear the wet and wind of a thunder-gust without tearing. To the top of the upright stick of the cross is to be fixed a very sharp-pointed wire, ris-

Human felicity is produced not so much
by great pieces of good fortune that seldom happen,
as by little advantages that occur every day.

The American Philosophical Society, another of Franklin's proposals, is housed in the building seen through the trees in this engraving, ca. 1779, by William Birch and Son. *(Historical Society of Pennsylvania)*

ing a foot or more above the wood. To the end of the twine, next the hand, is to be tied a silk ribbon, and where the silk and twine join, a key must be fastened. This kite is to be raised when a thunder-gust appears to be coming on, and the person who holds the string must stand within a door or window, or under some cover, so that the silk ribbon may not be wet; and care must be taken that the twine does not touch the frame of the door or window. As soon as any of the thunder-clouds come over the kite, the pointed wire will draw the electric fire from them, and the kite, with all the twine, will be electrified, and the loose filaments of the twine will stand out every way, and be attracted by an approaching finger. And when the rain has wet the kite and twine, so that it can conduct the electric fire freely, you will find it stream out plentifully from the key on the approach of your knuckle. At this key the phial may be charged; and from electric fire thus obtained, spirits may be kindled, and all the other electric experiments be performed, which are usually done by the help of a rubbed glass globe or tube, and thereby the sameness of the electric matter with that of lightning completely demonstrated.

B. Franklin

When the body is uneasy, the mind will be disturbed . . .

The Art of Procuring Pleasant Dreams
Inscribed to Miss [Shipley], being written at her request

As a great part of our life is spent in sleep during which we have sometimes pleasant and sometimes painful dreams, it becomes of some consequence to obtain the one kind and avoid the other; for whether real or imaginary, pain is pain and pleasure is pleasure. If we can sleep without dreaming, it is well that painful dreams are avoided. If while we sleep we can have any pleasing dream, it is, as the French say, *autant de gagné*, so much added to the pleasure of life.

To this end it is, in the first place, necessary to be careful in preserving health, by due exercise and great temperance; for, in sickness, the imagination is disturbed, and disagreeable, sometimes terrible, ideas are apt to present themselves. Exercise should precede meals, not immediately follow them; the first promotes, the latter, unless moderate, obstructs digestion. If, after exercise, we feed sparingly, the digestion will be easy and good, the body lightsome, the temper cheerful, and all the animal functions performed agreeably. Sleep, when it follows, will be natural and undisturbed; while indolence, with full feeding, occasions nightmares and horrors inexpressible; we fall from precipices, are assaulted by wild beasts, murderers, and demons, and experience every variety of distress. Observe, however, that the quantities of food and exercise are relative things; those who move much may, and indeed ought to eat more; those who use little exercise should eat little. In general, mankind, since the improvement of cookery, eat about twice as much as nature requires. . . .

Here, then, is one great and general cause of unpleasing dreams. For when the body is uneasy, the mind will be disturbed by it, and disagreeable ideas of various kinds will in sleep be the natural consequences. The remedies, preventive and curative, follow:

Franklin loved music and was quite accomplished at playing his invention, the (h)armonia, a musical instrument widely popular in Europe during his lifetime, though it later lost favor.
(Painting by A.Fostes; Bettmann Archive)

To have pleasant dreams take care to preserve a good conscience . . .

1. By eating moderately (as before advised for health's sake) less perspirable matter is produced in a given time; hence the bed-clothes receive it longer before they are saturated, and we may therefore sleep longer before we are made uneasy by their refusing to receive any more.

2. By using thinner and more porous bed-clothes, which will suffer the perspirable matter more easily to pass through them, we are less incommoded, such being longer tolerable.

3. When you are awakened by this uneasiness, and find you cannot easily sleep again, get out of bed, beat up and turn your pillow, shake the bed-clothes well, with at least twenty shakes, then throw the bed open and leave it to cool; in the meanwhile, continuing undressed, walk about your chamber till your skin has had time to discharge its load, which it will do sooner as the air may be dried and colder. When you begin to feel the cold air unpleasant, then return to your bed, and you will soon fall asleep, and your sleep will be sweet and pleasant. . . .

One or two observations more will conclude this little piece. Care must be taken, when you lie down, to displose your pillow so as to suit your manner of placing your head, and to be perfectly easy; then place your limbs so as not to bear inconveniently hard upon one another, as, for instance, the joints of your ankles; for, though a bad position may at first give but little pain and be hardly noticed, yet a continuance will render it less tolerable, and the uneasiness may come on while you are asleep, and disturb your imagination. These are the rules of the art. But, though they will generally prove effectual in producing the end intended, there is a case in which the most punctual observance of them will be totally fruitless. I need not mention the case to you, my dear friend, but my account of the art would be imperfect without it. The case is, when the person who desired to have pleasant dreams has not taken care to preserve, what is necessary above all things,

A Good Conscience.

What we call time enough
always proves little enough . . .

Above: A chair from Franklin's elegant home on High Street (now Market Street) is displayed at the Franklin Institute in Philadelphia. The portrait of Franklin is by Thomas Sully. *(Franklin Institute, Philadelphia.) Below:* A library chair with steps to assist a reader to reach high shelves was one of Franklin's most useful devices. *(American Philosophical Society)*

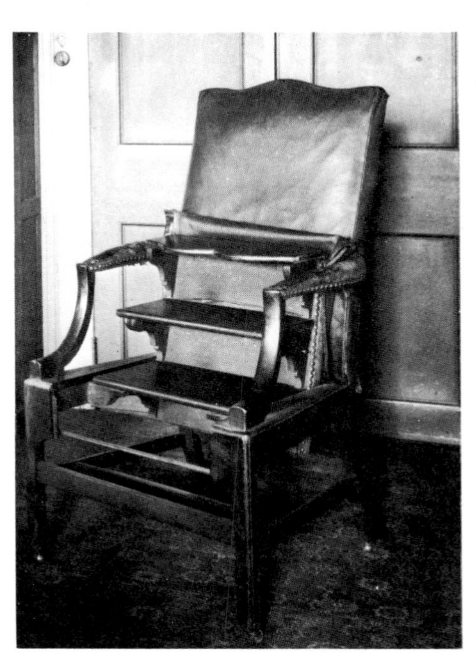

I shall never ask, never refuse, nor ever resign an office . . .

A profile medallion of Franklin by James Tassie, an artist employed in the English Wedgwood works. *(Scottish National Portrait Gallery)*

Benjamin Franklin Before the Lords Council, 1774, by R. Whitechurch, captures the grave turning point in Franklin's allegiance to Britain. After this denunciation, he felt there was no hope for reconciliation between American and English interests. *(Library of Congress)*

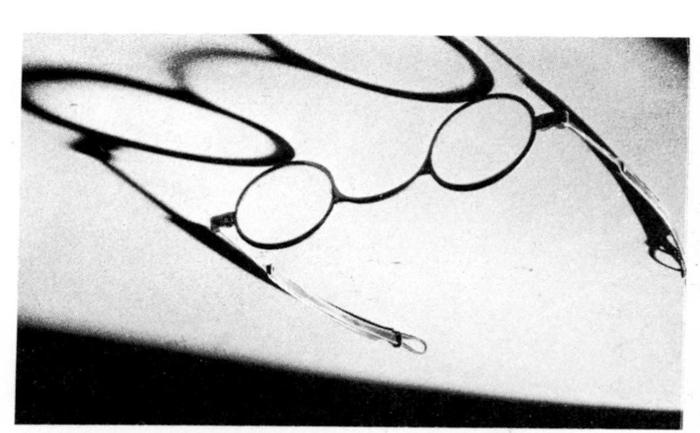

Franklin's regular glasses (not bifocals).
(Franklin Institute, Philadelphia)

Franklin watched with fascination many of the 1783 hot-air balloon ascensions in France, like this engraving of Peter de Rozier's and the Marquis d'Arlandes's ascent in the Garden of Versailles. *(Bettmann Archive)*

Let not the sun look down and say, inglorious here he lies . . .

From a letter to George Whatley, France, 1785

By Mr. Dollond's Saying, that my double Spectacles can only serve particular Eyes, I doubt he has not been rightly informed of their Construction. I imagine it will be found pretty generally true, that the same Convexity of Glass, through which a Man sees clearest and best at the Distance proper for Reading, is not the best for greater Distances. I therefore had formerly two Pair of Spectacles, which I shifted occasionally, as in travelling I sometimes read, and often wanted to regard the Prospects. Finding this Change troublesome, and not always sufficiently ready, I had the Glasses cut, and half of each kind associated in the same Circle. . . . By this means, as I wear my Spectacles constantly, I have only to move my Eyes up or down, as I want to see distinctly far or near, the proper Glasses being always ready. This I find more particularly convenient since my being in France, the Glasses that serve me best at Table to see what I eat, not being the best to see the Faces of those on the other Side of the Table who speak to me; and when one's Ears are not well accustomed to the Sounds of a Language, a Sight of the Movements in the Features of him that speaks helps to explain; so that I understand French better by the help of my Spectacles.

From a letter to Jan Ingenhousz on the hot-air balloon, France, 1784

It appears, as you observe, to be a discovery of great Importance, and what may possibly give a new turn to human Affairs. Convincing Sovereigns of the Folly of wars may perhaps be one

Considered an accurate likeness, this portrait of Franklin was painted by George D. Leslie after one by Mason Chamberlain. Franklin was 56 at this sitting.
(Yale University Art Gallery, gift of Avery Rockefeller)

Employ thy time well,
if thou meanest
to gain leisure . . .

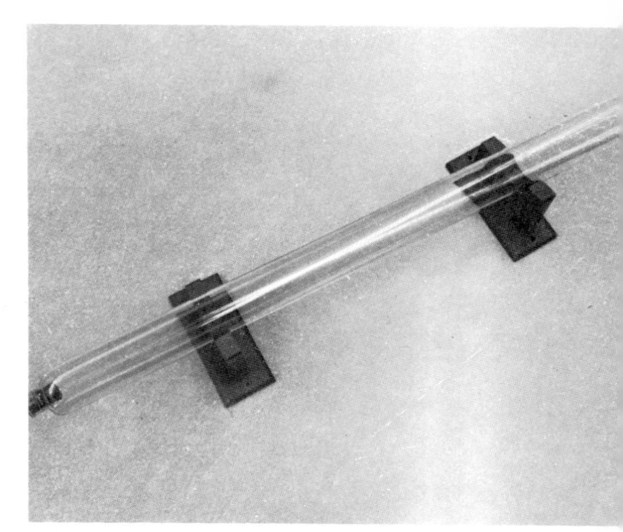

This glass tube was Peter Collinson's gift to Franklin, who used it frequently in his early electrical experiments to store or give charges.
(Franklin Institute, Philadelphia)

Effect of it; since it will be impracticable for the most potent of them to guard his Dominions. Five thousand Balloons, capable of raising two Men each, could not cost more than Five Ships of the Line; and where is the Prince who can afford so to cover his Country with Troops for its Defence, as that Ten Thousand Men descending from the Clouds might not in many places do an infinite deal of mischief, before a Force could be brought together to repel them? It is a pity that any national Jealously should, as you imagine it may, have prevented the English from prosecuting the Experiment, since they are such ingenious Mechanicians, that in their hands it might have made a more rapid progress towards Perfection, and all the Utility it is capable of affording.

From Experiments and Observations on Electricity
To Peter Collinson, 1747

Your kind present of an electric tube, with directions for using it, has put several of us on making electrical experiments, in which we have observed some particular phaenomena, that we look upon to be new. . . . For my own part, I never was before engaged in any study that so totally engrossed my attention and my time as this has lately done; for what with making experiments when I can be alone, and repeating them to my Friends and Acquaintance, who, from the novelty of the thing, come continually in crowds to see them, I have, during some months past, had little leisure for any thing else. . . .

B. Franklin

In the quarter century before the American Revolution, there was no other leading American so familiar with American and English needs and desires, so fond of each country and so eager to keep a happy, just union between the two as Franklin. He held onto his imperialist dreams for England in North America nearly until the Revolution. He cheered every British gain against the Spanish and French in the New World, and for a time envisioned America as the next seat of English power. And yet, from his extensive travels as Postmaster General throughout the colonies, he had first-hand knowledge of the increasing injustices in commerce and government.

The year 1757 proved to be a dividing line in Franklin's activities: He sailed to London as representative to Parliament and King George III from the Pennsylvania Assembly. He did not return home permanently until 1785.

His presence in London was a result of longstanding problems. First was the antagonism between the largely Quaker Assembly of Pennsylvania and the Proprietary Party (descendants of William Penn and their appointed governors) over taxation. The Penns refused to pay on their large estates, and, of course, the other merchants and landowners found this unacceptable. Franklin was sent to petition for royal assistance.

IV CITIZEN AND ADVOCATE

The second reason for sending Franklin to London was to increase support among sympathetic legislators in Parliament for jeopardized American civil rights. There was no thought at this time about independence, but there was discontent with government encroachments on civil liberties.

During his first stay in Britain (1757-62), Franklin also had leisure for some experimentation and travel to Scotland (1759), Belgium and Holland (1761) where he was well-received in scientific circles. His lodging at #7 Craven Street, Strand (London), owned by Mrs. Margaret Stevenson, became a second home for him. His friendship with her and her daughter Mary (Polly) was lifelong.

His return to America (1762-64) for two years is related in his letter to Lord Kames, a Scottish judge and notorious hoaxer like Franklin. During this time the Pennsylvania frontier exploded with Pontiac's Rebellion against encroaching white settlements and the Paxton Boys' reprisal against unrelated Indians. The armed Paxton Boys marched to Philadelphia to confront the predominantly Quaker Assembly which they blamed for being too lenient with the Indians. Franklin rode out to negotiate with the Paxton group. As he said, he was a very great man for about forty-eight hours when the Governor, John Penn, and the Assembly were frightened. After the fright passed, reprisals against Indians resumed, and John Penn proclaimed a bounty for Indian scalps. Franklin lost his Assembly seat in the election that followed. A majority of his supporters, however, remained in power, and he was elected to return to London to petition the King for a new colonial government.

Franklin sensed the uneasy times to come, though he remained hopeful and conciliatory until what is called the "Scene in the Cockpit." In

Congress Voting Independence, 1776, by Edward Savage shows Franklin an old man of 70, yet still in the thick of politics, as he had been for 40 years. *(Historical Society of Pennsylvania)*

1772, hoping to reconcile the Massachusetts populace with the King, he allowed private letters of the Massachusetts governor and lieutenant governor, Thomas Hutchinson and Andrew Oliver, to be circulated among friends in Boston. In these letters of 1768-69, Hutchinson and others, *Americans,* advocated military presence and suspension of English civil rights in the colonies as a means of keeping them in line. Franklin hoped that the colonists would see that their problems were not all with the English, but also with native Americans. Bostonians were outraged, and the Massachusetts House petitioned for Hutchinson's removal. Wild stories circulated on the means by which Franklin received the letters; two men dueled over it; Franklin refused to reveal his source, assuming all responsibility. London newspapers denounced him as an enemy to Britain's welfare, an incendiary. He was summoned by the Lords Council on Plantation Affairs to appear in the Cockpit (a Parliamentary chamber) while the Massachusetts petition was considered. What occurred there in January, 1774, was not a hearing but a one-sided diatribe by the Solicitor-General against Franklin personally, before many nobles and onlookers.

Unofficial negotiations continued in private with meetings between sympathetic Englishmen and Franklin, but the American terms he insisted upon were too stiff. Early in 1775 news arrived that Deborah Franklin had died the preceding December. Franklin had given up hope now that he and the sympathetic English could prevail against the King, Lord North and the majority of Parliament that Americans were enemies of the Empire. He returned to America, arriving shortly before the Battle of Bunker Hill (June 1775). Instead of resting, he became engulfed in the activities of ten committees of the Continental Congress.

The St. James Park that Franklin referred to in his satire on felons and rattlesnakes looked exactly like the above in 1751. Engraving by H. Roberts. *(Historical Pictures Service, Chicago)*

There is no human scheme so perfect . . .

Exporting of Felons to the Colonies

To the Printer of The Gazette:

By a Passage in one of your late Papers, I understand that the Government at home will not suffer our mistaken Assemblies to make any Law for preventing or discouraging the Importation of Convicts from Great Britain, for this kind Reason, *'That such laws are against the Publick Utility, as they tend to prevent the* Improvement *and* Well Peopling *of the Colonies.'*

Such a tender *parental* Concern in our Mother Country for the *Welfare* of her *Children,* calls aloud for the highest *Returns* of Gratitude and Duty. This every one must be sensible of: But 'tis said, that in our present Circumstances it is absolutely impossible for us to make *such* as are adequate to the Favour. I own it; but nevertheless let us do our Endeavour. 'Tis something to show a grateful Disposition.

In some of the uninhabited Parts of these Provinces, there are Numbers of these venomous Reptiles we call Rattlesnakes; Felons-convict from the Beginning of the World: These, whenever we meet with them, we put to Death, by Virtue of an old Law, *Thou shalt bruise his Head.* But as this is a sanguinary Law, and may seem too cruel; and as however mischievous those Creatures are with us, they may possibly change their Natures, if they were to change the Climate; I would humbly propose, that this general Sentence of *Death* be changed for *Transportation.*

A plan for the union of all colonies under one government . . .

In the Spring of the Year, when they first creep out of their Holes, they are feeble, heavy, slow, and easily taken; and if a small Bounty were allow'd *per* Head, some Thousands might be collected annually, and *transported* to *Britain.* There I would propose to have them carefully distributed in *St. James's Park,* in the *Spring-Gardens* and other Places of Pleasure about *London;* in the Gardens of all the Nobility and Gentry throughout the Nation; but particularly in the Gardens of the *Prime Ministers,* the *Lords of Trade* and *Members of Parliament;* for to them we are *most particularly* obliged. . . .

Thus it may perhaps be objected to my Scheme, that the *Rattle-Snake* is a mischievous Creature, and that his changing his Nature with the Clime is a mere Supposition, not yet confirm'd by sufficient Facts. What then? Is not Example more prevalent than Precept? And may not the honest rough British Gentry, by a Familiarity with these Reptiles, learn to *creep,* and to *insinuate,* and to *slaver,* and to *wriggle,* into Place (and perhaps to *poison* such as stand in their Way) Qualities of no small Advantage of Courtiers! In comparison of which 'Improvement and Publick Utility,' what is a *Child* now and then kill'd by their venomous Bite, . . . or even a favourite *Lap Dog?*

I would only add, that this exporting of Felons to the Colonies, may be consider'd as a *Trade,* as well as in the Light of a *Favour,* Now all Commerce implies Returns: Justice requires them: There can be no Trade without them. And *Rattle-Snakes* seem the most *suitable Returns* for the *Human Serpents* sent us by our *Mother* Country. In this, however, as in every other Branch of Trade, she will have the Advantage of us. She will reap *equal* Benefits without equal Risque of the Inconveniences and Dangers. For the *Rattle-Snake* gives Warning before he attempts his Mischief; which the Convict does not. I am *Yours, &c.*

Americanus.

Autobiography, *1788*

In 1754, war with France being again apprehended, a congress of commissioners from the different colonies was, by order of the Lords of Trade, to be assembled at Albany, there to confer with the chiefs of the Six Nations concerning the means of defending both their country and ours. . . .

In our way thither, I projected and drew a plan for the union of all the colonies under one government, so far as might be necessary for defense, and other important general purposes. . . it then appeared that several of the commissioners had form'd plans of the same kind. A previous question was first taken, whether a union should be established, which pass'd in the affirmative unanimously. A committee was then appointed, one member from each colony, to consider the several plans and report. Mine happen'd to be preferr'd, and, with a few amendments, was accordingly reported.

Franklin had an ivory miniature painted by C. Dixon in 1757 for his sister to wear. *(Museum of Fine Arts, Boston, gift of Franklin Greene Balch)*

The foundations of the future grandeur of the British empire lie in America . . .

From a letter to Lord Kames, *London, 1760*

No one can more sincerely rejoice than I do, on the reduction of Canada; and this is not merely as I am a colonist, but as I am a Briton. I have long been of opinion, that the *foundations of the future grandeur and stability of the British empire lie in America;* and though, like other foundations, they are low and little seen, they are, nevertheless, broad and strong enough to support the greatest political structure human wisdom ever yet erected. I am therefore by no means for restoring Canada. If we keep it, all the country from the St. Lawrence to the Mississippi will in another century be filled with British people. Britain itself will become vastly more populous, by the immense increase of its commerce; the Atlantic sea will be covered with your trading ships; and your naval power, thence continually increasing, will extend your influence round the whole globe, and awe the world! If the French remain in Canada, they will continually harass our colonies by the Indians, and impede if not prevent their growth; your progress to greatness will at best be slow,. . . .

The year 1760 saw the demise of French power in North America with the British victory at Quebec. This English cartoonist affirms Britain as the only rightful owner of northern North America, a view with which Franklin agreed. *(Library of Congress)*

Some Americans were preparing for independence when Franklin returned home after 11 years (1764-75) of representing colonial interests in London. Within a year, in 1776, independence was declared. An idealized *Raising of the Liberty Pole*, by John McRae pictures the event. *(Kennedy Galleries, New York)*

Attack on Bunker's Hill, with the Burning of Charles Town.
(National Gallery of Art, gift of Edgar William and Bernice Chrysler Garbisch)

The State House, Philadelphia, where the Declaration of Independence was adopted and the Constitution was drafted. From a drawing by Charles Willson Peale. *(Historical Society of Pennsylvania)*

The Liberty Bell was used on many occasions prior to and after its ringing at the public reading of the Declaration of Independence, July 8, 1776. It rang in 1757 when the Pennsylvania Assembly sent Franklin to England to seek redress of grievances and in 1765, 1768 and 1770 to protest taxation and other impositions by Parliament. It rang in 1783 to proclaim peace and in 1799 to toll Washington's death. It cracked and was repaired several times. Presently it is irreparable and hangs in the Pennsylvania State House called Independence Hall.

Ray Millman — Cyr Agency

Franklin was one of Pennsylvania's 25 delegates to the conference of the Committee of Safety in June 1776 that foreswore allegiance to the English king and which voted to form a constitution. The five who drew up the Declaration of Independence stand together in the center of this painting by an unknown artist: Adams, Sherman, Livingston, Jefferson and Franklin. Washington is seated on the right. On July 8, Franklin was elected president of the Constitutional Convention.
(Insurance Company of North America)

Can it be discreet to kick up in your own house a family quarrel? . . .

A Letter Concerning the Stamp Act

To the printer of the Gazetteer, *1766:*

Give me leave, Master John Bull, to remind you, that you are related to all mankind; and therefore it less becomes you than anybody, to affront and abuse other nations. But you have mixed with your many virtues a pride, a haughtiness, and an insolent contempt for all but yourself, that, I am afraid, will, if not abated, procure you one day or other a handsome drubbing. Besides your rudeness to foreigners, you are far from being civil even to your own family. . . . But, pray, when your enemies are uniting in a Family Compact against you, can it be discreet in you to kick up in your own house a Family Quarrel? And at the very time you are inviting foreigners to settle on your lands, and when you have more to settle than you had before, is it prudent to suffer your lawyer, Vindex, to abuse those who have settled there already, because they cannot yet speak "plain English?" — It is my opinion Master Bull, that the Scotch and Irish, as well as the Colonists are capable of speaking much plainer English that they ever yet spoke, but which I hope they will never be provoked to speak.

Homespun

Franklin arrived in France after a raw November voyage, so weak he could hardly stand and not yet expected by friends or the government. The British ambassador in France was certain he came to gain French aid, though other Britons hoped he was running away from a lost cause. It soon was apparent he came for and was gaining French support.

Arriving in 1777, in ordinary dress and fur cap to keep his head warm (most men in upper levels of French society wore powdered wigs), Franklin appeared to the French as the home-spun Quaker philosopher they had expected. "Poor Richard," as he was pictured by the middle and lower classes, was already familiar, for his *Way to Wealth* from the *Almanack* had been widely published in France. Soon, as one of Franklin's editors

V AMBASSADOR IN PARIS AND ELDER STATESMAN AT HOME

says, "The enthusiasm for *le grand Franklin* became a passion . . . idolatry." As a symbol of democracy, Franklin was deified in an unparalleled way.

Franklin made the best of this favor, for certainly the American cause needed all possible support. He kept the fur cap, unfashionable spectacles and thoroughly enjoyed being the primitive sage. His private letters show he was amused with seeing his image reproduced on plaques, snuffboxes, mugs, miniature paintings and the like. There is a story that King Louis XVI, tired of hearing a noblewoman's continual praise of Franklin, presented her with a chamberpot with his picture on the bottom. Despite all the adulation, however gratifying, Franklin remained aware of the quick changes of fortune he had endured as a public figure.

Congress depended on Franklin for French loans and good will. In addition to the official duties of the commissioner, Franklin found himself undertaking other responsibilities. He never received the secretary Congress promised, so he and his grandson kept the huge correspondence files. Franklin served as a judge of admiralty who commissioned privateers to harass and embarrass British merchants, judged the legality of captures, and ordered the prizes to be sold and distributed. Though he later despised privateering, these actions gave him some leverage in exchanging prisoners and gaining supplies.

Other endeavors were the improvement of prisoner-of-war conditions and purchase of military supplies. The most fatiguing work, he said, was accounting for all the bills of exchange Congress drew on its French bank account, for which Franklin alone secured eighteen million livres (over $3,600,000) by 1782. Without French aid (totaling over $8,000,000 by 1783), and thus without Franklin's work in France, the Revolutionary War would not have succeeded.

An allegorical engraving, ca. 1778, by Etienne Palliere, of Franklin's arrival in France shows him as he was popularly recognized, in fur cap and glasses. Louis XVI is the figure to his right in armor. Various pagan gods prepare armaments, others make thunder, and another saves a distressed woman (presumably American) from the British lion. *(Yale University Art Gallery, William Smith Mason Collection)*

In his final public service in France, Franklin worked with John Jay, John Adams, Henry Laurens and Thomas Jefferson in successfully concluding peace negotiations with England in September of 1783, about one year after the British surrender at Yorktown. Franklin had been continually in touch with Englishmen who also hoped to end the war, but declined all their early offers for a separate peace, excluding France. It was essential that America have equal commerical and political rights with all Europeans.

His last two years in America were spent in retirement and waning health with his daughter and among friends. Alert to the end, his interest in science continued, as did interest in the affairs of his new nation and the upheavals in France. The effects of pleurisy when he was young finally took effect on his weakened body; an abscess in his lungs broke, he nearly suffocated, then fell into a coma. He died April 17, 1790, at eighty-four.

Ben Franklin's Belles, by Norman Rockwell. Among the talented women of France who became Franklin's social companions were duchesses, countesses and ladies whose fame rested in ability as writers, wits, mistresses and musicians and in what the French call the *joi de vivre*, "joy of living." *(Collection of Mr. Joseph Hennage)*

Must a man afford himself no leisure? . . .

From a letter to Mrs. Thompson, Paris, 1777

. . . I know you wish you could see me; but, as you can't, I will describe myself to you. Figure me in your mind as jolly as formerly, and as strong and hearty, only a few years older; very plainly dress'd, wearing my thin gray strait hair, that peeps out under my only *Coiffure*, a fine Fur Cap, which comes down my Forehead almost to my Spectacles. Think how this must appear among the Powder'd Heads of Paris! I wish every gentleman and Lady in France would only be so obliging as to follow my Fashion, comb their own Heads as I do mine, dismiss their *Friseurs*, and pay me half the Money they paid to them. You see, the gentry might well afford this, and I could then enlist those *Friseurs*, who are at least 100,000, and with the Money I would maintain them, make a Visit with them to England, and dress the Heads of your Ministers and Privy Counsellors; which I conceive to be at present *un peu dérangées* ["a little disturbed"]. Adieu, Madcap; and believe me ever, your affectionate Friend and humble Servant,

B. Franklin

From a letter to Mrs. Elizabeth Partridge, France, 1779

You mention the Kindness of the French Ladies to me. I must explain that matter. This is the civilest nation upon Earth. Your first Acquaintances endeavour to find out what you like, and they tell others. If 'tis understood that you like Mutton, dine where you will you find Mutton. Somebody, it seems, gave it out that I lov'd Ladies; and then every body presented me their Ladies (or the Ladies presented themselves) to be *embrac'd*, that is to have their Necks kiss'd. For as to kissing of Lips or Cheeks it is not the Mode here, the first, is reckon'd rude, & the other may rub off the Paint. The French Ladies have however 1000 other ways of rendering themselves agreeable; by their various Attentions and Civilities, & their sensible Conversation. 'Tis a delightful People to live with.

[Dr. Samuel Cooper, of Boston, was an old friend of Franklin who shared political and scientific interests. —Ed.]

From a letter to Samuel Cooper, Paris, 1777

I rejoice with you in the happy Change of Affairs in America last Winter. I hope the same Train of Success will continue thro' the Summer. Our Enemies are disappointed in the Number of additional Troops they purposed to send over. What they have been able to muster will not probably recruit their Army to the State it was in the beginning of last Campaign; and ours I hope will be equally numerous, better arm'd, and better clothed, than they have been heretofore.

They read our separate colony constitutions with rapture . . .

All Europe is on our Side of the Question, as far as Applause and good Wishes can carry them. Those who live under arbitrary Power do nevertheless approve of Liberty, and wish for it; they almost despair of recovering it in Europe; they read the Translations of our separate Colony Constitutions with Rapture; and there are such Numbers everywhere, who talk of Removing to America, with their Families and Fortunes, as soon as Peace and our Independence shall be established, that 'tis generally believed we shall have a prodigious Addition of Strength, Wealth, and Arts, from the Emigrations of Europe; and 'tis thought, that, to lessen or prevent such Emigrations, the Tyrannies established there must relax, and allow more Liberty to their People. Hence 'tis a Common Observation here, that our Cause is *the Cause of all Mankind*, and that we are fighting for their Liberty in defending our own. 'Tis a glorious tasked assigned'd us by Providence; which has, I trust, given us Spirit and Virtue equal to it, and will at last crown it with Success. I am ever, my dear Friend, yours most affectionately,

B. F[ranklin].

To Mrs. Sarah Franklin Bache, France, 1779

Dear Sally: I have before me your letters of October 22d and January 17th. They are the only ones I received from you in the course of eighteen months. If you knew how happy your letters make me, and considered how many miscarry, I think you would write oftener. . . .

The clay medallion of me you say you gave to Mr. Hopkinson was the first of the kind made in France. A variety of others have been made since of different sizes; some to be set in the lids of snuff-boxes, and some so small as to be worn in rings; and the numbers sold are incredible. These, with the pictures, busts, and prints, (of which copies upon copies are spread everywhere,) have made your father's face as well known as that of the moon, so that he durst not

Opposite: Franklin's fur cap and glasses were considered sensational when he appeared thus dressed as New World ambassador. This 1777 engraving was reworked on countless items like watches, prints and medallions. Etched by A. de Saint Aubin after a drawing by C.N. Cochin.
(The Philadelphia Museum of Art)

BENJAMIN FRANKLIN.
Né à Boston, dans la nouvelle Angleterre le 17. Janvier 1706.
Dessiné par C. N. Cochin Chevalier de l'Ordre du Roi, en 1777 et Gravé par Aug. de St. Aubin Graveur de la Bibliotheque du Roi.
Se vend à Paris chés C. N. Cochin aux Galleries du Louvre ; et chés Aug. de St. Aubin, rue des Mathurins.

Be ashamed to catch yourself idle . . .

do any thing that would oblige him to run away, as his phiz would discover him wherever he should venture to show it. It is said by learned etymologists, that the name *doll,* for the images children play with, is derived from the word Idol. From the number of *dolls* now made of him, he may be truly said, *in that sense,* to be *i-doll-ized* in this country. . . .

I was charmed with the account you gave me of your industry, the tablecloths of your own spinning, &c.; but the latter part of the paragraph, that you had sent for linen from France, because weaving and flax were grown dear, alas, that dissolved the charm; and your sending for long black pins, and lace, and feathers! disgusted me as much as if you had put salt into my strawberries. The spinning, I see, is laid aside, and you are to be dressed for the ball! You seem not to know, my dear daughter, that, of all the dear things in this world, idleness is the dearest, except mischief. . . .

When I began to read your account of the high prices of goods," a pair of gloves, $7; a yard of common gauze, $24, and that it now required a fortune to maintain a family in a very plain way," I expected you would conclude with telling me, that everybody as well as yourself was grown frugal and industrious; and I could scarce believe my eyes in reading forward, that "there never was so much pleasure and dressing going on;" and that you yourself wanted black pins and feathers from France to appear, I suppose, in the mode! . . . The War indeed may in some degree raise the prices of goods, and the high taxes which are necessary to support the war may make our frugality necessary; and, as I am always preaching that doctrine, I cannot in conscience or in decency encourage the contrary, by my example, in furnishing my children with foolish modes and luxuries. I therefore send all the articles you desire, that are useful and necessary, and omit the rest; for, as you say you should "have great pride in wearing any thing I send, and showing it as your father's taste," I must avoid giving you an opportunity of doing that with either lace or feathers. If you wear your cambric ruffles as I do, and take care not to mend the holes, they will come in time to be lace; and feathers, my dear girl, may be had in America from every cock's tail. . . .

Present my affectionate regards to all friends that inquire after me . . . and write oftener, my dear child, to your loving father,

B. Franklin

Opposite: David Martin's "Thumb Portrait" of Franklin was painted in 1766. *(The White House, gift of Mr. and Mrs. Walter H. Annenberg)*

The industrious country that Franklin wanted America to be was epitomized in its leading city, Philadelphia. Pictured is the New Market at the corner of Shippen and Second streets *(Courtesy, The New-York Historical Society)*

From the Comparison of Great Britain and the United States in Regard to the Basis of Credit in the Two Countries, *1777*

In rivers and bad government, the lightest things swim a top . . .

With regard to Frugality in Expences; the Manner of Living in America is in general more simple and less Expensive than in England. Plain Tables, plain Clothing, plain Furniture in Houses, few Carriages of Pleasure. In America an expensive Appearance hurts Credit, and is therefore avoided; in England it is often put on with a View of gaining Credit, and continued to Ruin. In *publick* Affairs, the Difference is still greater. In England Salaries of Officers and Emoluments of office are Enormous. The King has a Million Sterling per Annum, and yet cannot maintain his Family free of Debt; Secretaries of State, Lords of the Treasury, Admiralty, &c., have vast Appointments. . . . This is all paid by the People, who are oppress'd by the Taxes so occasioned, and thereby rendered less able to contribute to the Payment of necessary national Debts. In America, Salaries, where indispensable, are extreamly low; but much of publick Business is done gratis. The Honour of serving the Publick ably and faithfully is deemed sufficient. *Public Spirit* really exists there, and has great Effects. In England it is universally deemed a NonEntity, and whoever pretends to it is laugh'd at as a fool, or suspected as a Knave. The Committees of Congress . . . all attend the Business of their respective Functions without any Salary or Emolument whatever, tho' they spend in it much more of their Time, than any Lord of Treasury or Admiralty in England can afford from his Amusements. . . .

A portrait of John Paul Jones (1747-92), by J. M. Moreau the Younger, was made soon after his brilliant naval victory against the English in 1779. *(Louisiana State Museum, New Orleans)*

In this world nothing is certain but death and taxes . . .

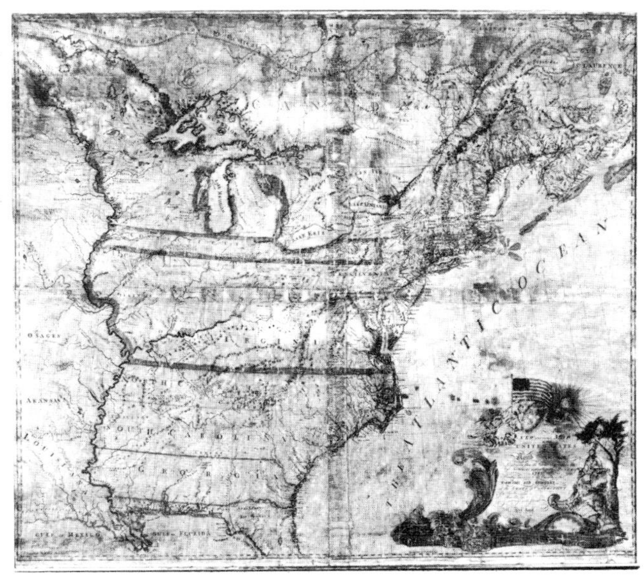

The first map of the United States, 1783, engraved by Abel Buel. *(I. N. Phelps Stokes Collection, Prints Division, New York Public Library, Astor, Lenox and Tilden Foundations)*

[*Franklin wrote this in response to what is now the famous battle between John Paul Jones's* Bonhomme Richard *and the English* Serapis *and* Countess of Scarborough, *in which the* Bonhomme Richard *was so badly battered that it sank after several days. —Ed.*]

From a letter to John Paul Jones, France, 1779

Dear Sir: I received the Account of your Cruise and Engagement with the *Serapis*, which you did me the honour to send me from the Texel. I have since received your Favor of the 8th, from Amsterdam. For some Days after the Arrival of your Express, scarce any thing was talked of at Paris and Versailles, but your cool Conduct and persevering Bravery during that terrible Conflict. You may believe, that the Impression on my Mind was not less strong than on that of others; but I do not choose to say in a letter to yourself all I think on such an Occasion.

Franklin's Reception in the Court of France, 1778, by J. Smith. Louis XVI and Marie Antoinette are the seated figures. *(Library of Congress)*

A Limoge china tea set given to Franklin in France and used by him in Philadelphia. *(Franklin Institute, Philadelphia)*

We are all men, all subject to errors . . .

From a letter to George Washington, France, 1780

Should peace arrive after another Campaign or two, and afford us a little Leisure, I should be happy to see your Excellency in Europe, and to accompany you, if my Age and Strength would permit, in visiting some of its ancient and most famous Kingdoms. You would, on this side of the Sea, enjoy the great Reputation you have acquir'd, pure and free from those little Shades that the Jealousy and Envy of a Man's Countrymen and Cotemporaries are ever endeavouring to cast over living Merit. Here you would know, and enjoy, what Posterity will say of Washington. For 1000 Leagues have nearly the same Effect with 1000 Years. The feeble Voice of those grovelling Passions cannot extend so far either in Time or Distance. At present I enjoy that Pleasure for you, as I frequently hear the old Generals of this martial Country, (who study the Maps of America, and mark upon them all your Operations,) speak with sincere Approbation and great Applause of your conduct; and join in giving you the Character of one of the greatest Captains of the Age.

I must soon quit the Scene, but you may live to see our Country flourish, as it will amazingly and rapidly after the War is over. Like a Field of young Indian Corn, which long Fair weather and Sunshine had enfeebled and discolored, and which in that weak State, by a Thunder Gust, of violent Wind, Hail, and Rain, seem'd to be threaten'd with absolute Destruction; yet the Storm being past, it recovers fresh Verdure, shoots up with double Vigour, and delights the Eye, not of its Owner only, but of every observing Traveller.

[*Washington never took up Franklin's offer to visit Europe. —Ed.*]

From a letter to William Franklin, France, 1784

Dear Son: I received your Letter of the 22d past, and am glad to find that you desire to revive the affectionate Intercourse, that formerly existed between us. It will be very agreeable to me; indeed nothing has ever hurt me so much and affected me with such keen Sensations, as to find myself deserted in my old Age by my only Son; and not only deserted, but to find him taking up Arms against me, in a Cause, wherein my good Fame, Fortune and Life were all at Stake. You conceived, you say, that your Duty to your King and Regard for your Country requir'd this. I ought not to blame you for differing in Sentiment with me in Public Affairs. We are Men, all subject to Errors. Our Opinions are not in our own Power; they are form'd and govern'd much by Circumstances, that are often as inexplicable as they are irresistible. Your Situation was such that few would have censured your remaining Neuter, *tho' there are Natural Duties which precede political ones, and cannot be extinguish'd by them.*

Unfailing wit was part of Franklin's success as a writer. His *Gazette* and *Poor Richard's Almanack* were filled with facetious predictions, tales and editorial comments that gained him immediate popularity.

Franklin's spontaneous humor and the joys he found in friends and family and his playful intrigues with women deserve special attention. There has been much speculation about Franklin's feelings toward his wife, Deborah. Franklin's marriage, though it lacks all the romance that makes good stories, was a long and contented one. Excluding the year preceding Deborah's death (she was ill and lonely while Franklin negotiated in London), their affection never failed.

Much more has been made of Franklin's relationships with other women: the early intrigues he so regretted; his feelings for Catherine Ray, a coy, young relation; his affection for Polly Stevenson, the daughter of

VI PHILOSOPHER, FRIEND AND HUMORIST

his English landlady, and her girlfriends; for the daughters of his friends, such as Georgina Shipley; and of course, to his fondness for many women friends in France, especially Mesdames Brillon and Helvétius. Warmth and intimacy are the tone of all Franklin's private letters, to men or women, boys or girls; his paternalistic style has been amusingly interpreted at times, and literal-minded biographers have counted some of his young friends, whom he would call "my daughter," as his offspring. This is not to deny his early affairs (mentioned in the *Autobiography*), his delight in women's company, or relish for playing the witty love games of words and suggestions so enjoyed in the cultured eighteenth-century France and England. Yet Franklin, by the time he was twenty-four, had come to respect marriage as the happiest state because it was the healthiest. He encouraged his young friends, such as Polly Stevenson and Catherine Ray, to find good mates for themselves, though he teased Catherine and cheerfully pleaded that she unfairly refused his offer to teach her "multiplication and addition," according to the rules of their word game.

In France, his two most intimate friends were Anne-Louise Brillon and Anne-Catherine Helvétius. Franklin was a widower whose family lived across an ocean. Madame Helvétius was widowed, thirteen years younger than Franklin, independent and bohemian. Madame Brillon was a recognized musician, an intellect and many years younger than her prosaic, philandering husband. The comforts of Madame Brillon's home — young children to remind him of his own grandchildren, good music, dinners, chess and agreeable conversation — were a restorative to Franklin. She revered and loved him as she had her late father, and he was elated to have a "daughter" so accomplished. Yet, in their letters it appears that Franklin's gallantry had a serious import, though Madame Brillon insisted that their pleasures together would have to be reserved for

A whimsical-looking Franklin is preserved in the 1790 aquatint by Pierre Michel Alix after a painting by L. M. Vanloo.
(The Philadelphia Museum of Art)

paradise. He implored Christian charity, and she referred him to philosphy: ". . . the gentleman, great philospher that he is, goes by the doctrines of Anacreon (writer of love poems) and Epicure (devotee of sensual pleasure), but the lady is a Platonist."

At Madame Helvétius' country estate, he found a more madcap existence, stimulating and intellectual, though Madame was more an exuberant individualist than an intellect. Madame Helvétius was once beautiful and still retained regal bearing when Franklin met her. He was openly devoted to her and proposed marriage. She refused, in deference to the memory of her late husband, she said.

A final and significant aspect of Franklin's private life is his feeling and writing on religion. A letter to a Philadelphia friend restates his constant belief: "If men rest in Hearing and Praying, as all too many do, it is as if a Tree should Value itself without being watered and putting forth many Leaves, tho' it never produced any Fruit."

Franklin looks like a stern moralist in this painting by Joseph Wright, though in fact he was apt to forgive readily his own and others' faults. *(The Pennsylvania Academy of the Fine Arts, Joseph and Sarah Harrison Collection)*

Franklin's image, which artists portrayed with as many faces as the moon, looks surprisingly unheroic in this French 1783 pencil sketch. *(Walters Art Gallery)*

[Franklin composed many facetious letters from "readers" like Alice Addertongue, Celia Single and Anthony Afterwit to entertain and gain subscribers to his Gazette. *Addertongue made a strong defense of scandal as* censure *done for the good of her country-folk. —Ed.]*

It seems that happiness in this life rather depends on internals than externals . . .

From a letter from Alice Addertongue

Printed in The Pennsylvania Gazette, *1732*

. . . 'Tis a Principle with me, that none ought to have a greater Share of Reputation, than they really deserve; if they have, 'tis an Imposition upon the Publick. I know it is every one's Interest, and therefore believe they endeavour to conceal all their Vices and Follies; and I hold that those People are *extraordinary* foolish or careless, who suffer a Fourth of their Failings to come to publick Knowledge. Taking then the common Prudence and Imprudence of Mankind in a Lump, I suppose none suffer above *one Fifth* to be discovered: Therefore, when I hear of any person's Misdoing, I think I keep within Bounds if in relating it I only make it *three times* worse than it is; and I reserve to myself the Privilege of charging them with one Fault in four, which for aught I know, they may be entirely innocent of. You see there are but few so careful of doing Justice as myself. What Reason then have Mankind to complain of *Scandal*? In a general way the worst that is said of us is only half of what *might* be said, if all our Faults were seen.

Franklin as he is most fondly thought of: reading his own words to the wise from an *Almanack* and sitting beside his stove. *(Courtesy of John Hancock Mutual Life Insurance Company)*

A finely detailed Franklin medallion, by J. B. Nini, 1777. *(Courtesy, Henry Francis du Pont Winterthur Museum)*

The "rising sun" chair was used by Washington as President of the Constitutional Convention. At the signing of the document, Franklin commented that finally he was certain that the figure symbolized for America a rising, not a setting, sun.
(Independence National Historical Park)

Signing of the Constitution of the United States, by Howard C. Christy, hangs in the U. S. Capitol, in the House of Representatives. Washington presides, and Franklin sits in the foreground. His speech of reconciliation over representation did much to assure the Constitution would be adopted unanimously. *(Franklin Institute, Philadelphia)*

From a letter to Madame Brillon, France, 1779

The Whistle

The miseries of mankind are brought upon by false estimates of value . . .

I am charmed with your description of Paradise, and with your plan of living there; and I approve much of your conclusion, that, in the mean time, we should draw all the good we can from this world. In my opinion, we might all draw more good from it than we do, and suffer less evil, if we would take care not to give too much for *whistles*. For to me it seems, that most of the unhappy people we meet with, are become so by neglect of that caution.

You ask what I mean? You love stories, and will excuse my telling one of myself.

When I was a child of seven years old, my friends, on a holiday, filled my pockets with coppers. I went directly to a shop where they sold toys for children; and, being charmed with the sound of a *whistle*, that I met by the way in the hands of another boy, I voluntarily offered and gave all my money for one. I then came home, and went whistling all over the house, much pleased with my *whistle*, but disturbing all the family. My brothers, and sisters, and cousins, understanding the bargain I had made, told me I had given four times as much for it as it was worth; put me in mind what good things I might have bought with the rest of the money; and laughed at me so much for my folly, that I cried with vexation; and the reflection gave me more chagrin than the *whistle* gave me pleasure.

This however was afterwards of use to me, the impression continuing on my mind; so that often, when I was tempted to buy some unnecessary thing, I said to myself, *Don't give too much for the whistle;* and I saved my money.

As I grew up, came into the world, and observed the actions of men, I thought I met with many, very many, who *gave too much for the whistle*. . . .

When I saw another fond of popularity, constantly employing himself in political bustles, neglecting his own affairs, and ruining them by that neglect, *He pays, indeed,* said I, *too much for his whistle.*

If I knew a miser, who gave up every kind of comfortable living, all the pleasures of doing good to others, all the esteem of his fellow-citizens, and the joys of benevolent friendship, for the sake of accumulating wealth, *Poor man,* said I, *you pay too much for your whistle.*

When I met with a man of pleasure, sacrificing every laudable improvement of the mind, or of his fortune, to mere corporeal sensations, and ruining his health in their pursuit, *Mistaken man,* said I, *you are providing pain for yourself, instead of pleasure; you give too much for your whistle.*

If I see one fond of appearance, or fine clothes, fine houses, fine furniture, fine equipages, all above his fortune, for which he contracts debts, and ends his career in a prison, *Alas!* say I, *he has paid dear, very dear, for his whistle.*

When I see a beautiful, sweet-tempered girl married to an ill-natured brute of a husband, *What a pity*, say I, *that she should pay so much for a whistle!*

In short, I conceive that great part of the miseries of mankind are brought upon them by the false estimates they have made of the value of things, and by their *giving too much for their whistles.*

Diogenes, the ancient Greek philosopher who in legend searched for a real man, reveals Franklin as his discovery in this 1780 French print. *(American Philosophical Society)*

Above: One of the finest examples of Bristol porcelain used in a portrait plaque is this of Franklin, ca. 1777, which he owned for a time. *(British Museum)*

Opposite: A marble bust of Franklin, done with very delicate craftsmanship by J. A. Houdon, 1780. *(William Rockhill Nelson Gallery of Art, Atkins Museum of Fine Arts)*

The most acceptable service of God is the doing good to man . . .

A silver tankard with the Franklin coat of arms, owned and probably used by Franklin. *(Franklin Institute, Philadelphia)*

Autobiography, *France, 1784*

I had been religiously educated as a Presbyterian; and tho' some of the dogmas of that persuasion, such as *the eternal decrees of God, election, reprobation, etc.,* appeared to me unintelligible, others doubtful, and I early absented myself from the public assemblies of the sect, Sunday being my studying day, I never was without some religious principles. I never doubted, for instance, the existence of the Deity; that he made the world, and govern'd it by his Providence; that the most acceptable service of God was the doing good to man; that our souls are immortal; and that all crime will be punished, and virtue rewarded, either here or hereafter. These I esteem'd the essentials of every religion; and, being to be found in all the religions we had in our country, I respected them all, tho' with different degrees of respect, as I found them more or less mix'd with other articles, which, without any tendency to inspire, promote, or confirm morality, serv'd principally to divide us, and make us unfriendly to one another. This respect to all, with an opinion that the worst had some good effects, induc'd me to avoid all discourse that might tend to lessen the good opinion another might have of his own religion; and as our province increas'd in people, and new places of worship were continually wanted, and generally erected by voluntary contribution, my mite for such purpose, whatever might be the sect, was never refused.

. . . I had some years before compos'd a little Liturgy, or form of prayer, for my own private use (viz., in 1728), entitled, *Articles of Belief and Acts of Religion.* I return'd to the use of this, and went no more to the public assemblies. My conduct might be blameable, but I leave it, without attempting further to excuse it; my present purpose being to relate facts, and not to make apologies for them.

Right: Christ Church, Philadelphia, was an early landmark completed in 1744. Inside, a pew is marked with Franklin's name, and he is buried outside in the churchyard. Painting by William Strickland, 1811. *(Courtesy, Christ Church, Philadelphia)*

Below: "View of Several Public Buildings in Philadelphia, 1790," from the *Columbian Magazine.* From the left are, 1, the Episcopal Academy; 2, Congress Hall; 3, the State House; 4, the American Philosophical Society Hall; 5, Library Company of Philadelphia; 6, Carpenter's Hall. *(Historical Society of Pennsylvania)*

They that won't be counselled, can't be helped . . .

Dialogue between Franklin and the Gout, *1780*

Franklin. Eh! Oh! Eh! What have I done to merit these cruel sufferings?

Gout. Many things; you have ate and drank too freely, and too much indulged those legs of yours in their indolence.

Franklin. Who is it that accuses me?

Gout. It is I, even I, the Gout.

Franklin. What! my enemy in person?

Gout. No, not your enemy.

Franklin. I repeat it; my enemy; for you would not only torment my body to death, but ruin my good name; you reproach me as a glutton and a tippler; now all the world, that knows me, will allow that I am neither the one nor the other.

Gout. The world may think as it pleases; it is always very complaisant to itself, and sometimes to its friends; but I very well know that the quantity of meat and drink proper for a man, who takes a reasonable degree of exercise, would be too much for another, who never takes any.

. . . If your situation in life is a sedentary one, your amusements, your recreations, at least, should be active. You ought to walk or ride; or, if the weather prevents that, play at billiards. But let us examine your course of life. While the mornings are long, and you have leisure to go abroad, what do you do? Why, instead of gaining an appetite for breakfast, by salutary exercise, you amuse yourself, with books, pamphlets, or newspapers, which commonly are not worth the reading. . . .

Franklin. I am convinced now of the justness of poor Richard's remark, that "Our debts and our sins are always greater than we think for."

Gout. So it is. Your philosophers are sages in your maxims, and fools in your conduct. . . .

Franklin. Ah! how tiresome you are!

Gout. Well, then, to my office; it should not be forgotten that I am your physician. There.

Franklin. Ohhh! what a devil of a physician.

Gout. How ungrateful you are to say so! Is it not I who, in the character of your physician, have saved you from the palsy, dropsy, and apoplexy? One or other of which would have done for you long ago, but for me.

Franklin. I submit, and thank you for the past, but entreat the discontinuance of your visits for the future; for, in my mind, one had better die than be cured so dolefully. . . .

Oh! Oh! — for Heaven's sake leave me! and I promise faithfully never more to play at chess, but to take exercise daily, and live temperately.

Gout. I know you too well. You promise fair; but, after a few months of good health, you will return to your old habits; your fine promises will be forgotten like the forms of last year's clouds. Let us then finish the account, and I will go. But I leave you with an assurance of visiting you again at a proper time and place; for my object is your good, and you are sensible that I am your *real friend.*

The *"Fur Collar" Portrait* of Franklin, 1778, by J. S. Duplessis, was copied many times by the artist and other painters and often freely adapted. Franklin said this image of him was as familiar as the moon and as changeable. *(The Metropolitan Museum of Art, Michael Friedsam Collection)*

The pleasing consolation to know that you have not lived in vain . . .

"He seized fire from the heavens and sceptor from tyrants" — [*Eripuit caelo fulmen sceptrumque tyrannis*] — A. R. J. Turgot's famous epigram on Franklin may seem too sublime praise for a man who was altogether down to earth. Yet, to political leaders, scientists and the populace of eighteenth-century Europe, he was America's most eminent scientist and living symbol of democracy. To the newly made American nation, he must have been a stronghold of sensibility and harmony, always available for

EPILOGUE

service or advice. To two of the younger men we now call Founding Fathers, George Washington and Thomas Jefferson, he was always "the good old Doctor." A last letter from Washington is included in this chapter as a kind tribute to Franklin's generosity of spirit. To modern historians and readers, Franklin is still approachable and certainly more vulnerable than other American leaders of the time.

To Philadelphians, he was a well-known figure for over a half century, active in most political events and instigator of social benefits that made the city among the most progressive in America. At his death in 1790, it has been said that no other town burying its great man ever buried more of itself than Philadelphia with Franklin. An estimated twenty thousand people attended his funeral. The House of Representatives, hearing of Franklin's death, unanimously passed James Madison's motion that members wear the badge of mourning for one month.

Perhaps the most moving and fitting piece is from Franklin's own hand; the epitaph he composed in 1728 and often rewrote for friends from memory. It is prophetic, though Franklin hardly anticipated the degree of lettering and gilding the world would bestow on him. It shows that ease and confidence which prevailed throughout the "corrections" meeted out to him in his life.

In America after his death, historians' and popular regard for Franklin fluxuated with the mode. His straightforwardness in gaining material comfort, particularly in viewing political, religious and social conventions, and general tolerance and cheerfulness were often unpopular in the century following his time. His outlook was perhaps too healthy and happy to appeal to Romanticists, somewhat too materialistic or pragmatic to appeal to New England Transcendentalists, and generally too openly liberal and cosmopolitan for Victorian America. In recent decades Franklin has come to be better understood and admired as his life has been studied more.

Philadelphians had prospered during Franklin's lifetime, in part from his civic proposals for bettering the city, and had time for leisurely outings like this on the Schuylkill River. *(Courtesy, The New-York Historical Society)*

From a letter from George Washington

Would to God, my dear sir, that I could congratulate you upon the removal of that excruciating pain under which you labor, and that your existence might close with as much ease to yourself as its continuance has been beneficial to our country and useful to mankind; or, if the united wishes of a free people, joined with the earnest prayers of every friend to science and humanity, could relieve the body from pain or infirmities, that you could claim an exemption on this score. But this cannot be, and you have within yourself the only resource to which we can confidently apply for relief, a philosophic mind.

If to be venerated for benevolence, if to be admired to talents, if to be esteemed for patriotism, if to be beloved for philanthropy, can gratify the human mind, you must have the pleasing consolation to know that you have not lived in vain. And I flatter myself that it will not be ranked among the least grateful occurrences of your life to be assured that, so long as I retain my memory, you will be recollected with respect, veneration, and affection by your sincere friend,

George Washington

Several decades after Franklin's death and the execution of his will for benefitting his two homes cities, Boston and Philadelphia, Boston was in its prime as a maritime center as shown in this painting by Robert Salmon.
(U. S. Naval Academy Museum)

The epitaph Franklin composed in 1728 (version at Yale)

The Body of
B. Franklin,
Printer;
Like the Cover of an old Book,
Its Contents torn out,
And stript of its Lettering and Gilding,
Lies here, Food for Worms.
But the Work shall not be wholly lost;
For it will, as he believed, appear once more,
In a new and more perfect Edition,
Corrected and amended
By the Author.
He was born Jan. 6, 1706
Died 17—